What Baptists Believe and Practice

By Rev. R. H. Boyd, D.D., LL.D.

R.H. BOYD
EST. 1896

Classic Series

What Baptists Believe and Practice
Rev. R. H. Boyd, D.D., LL.D.

R.H. BOYD PUBLISHING CORPORATION
6717 Centennial Blvd.
Nashville, TN 37209-1049
www.rhboyd.com
1-877-4RHBOYD

ISBN: 978-1-58942-064-9

All Scripture quotations, unless otherwise noted, are taken from the *King James Version* of the Bible or are the author's paraphrase of it.

Printed in the United Stated of America.

"Beloved, when I have all diligence to write unto you of the common salvation, it was needful for me to write unto you, and exhort you that ye should earnestly contend for the faith which was once delivered unto the saints." (Jude 3)

"If ye love me, keep my commandments."
(John 14:15)

Rev. R.H. Boyd, D.D., LL.D.
Founder, National Baptist Publishing Board
1896–1922

CONTENTS

INTRODUCTION

The importance of clarifying what Baptists believe and practice grows upon us each day. In days of tremendous advancements in art, literature, the sciences, travel, and instant communication causing the world to grow small, there seems to be among Protestants an agreement upon a common understanding of God's Word.

There is indeed danger that the fundamental principles and old landmark doctrines, for which they have bled and died, will be forgotten by the upcoming generation as they engage in their various pursuits.

This little booklet is intended as a brief manual of beliefs and practices of the regular Baptist churches, as taught in the sacred Scriptures. Baptists draw no lines between essential and non-essential when they come to obey the commands of their Lord and Saviour Jesus Christ. They do not believe and cannot agree with many of their Christian friends that something else will do as well.

Christ said to His disciples, "Ye are my friends, if ye do whatsoever I command you." He said to them again, "If ye love me, keep my commandments." It is not enough for a converted soul and obedient heart to ask,

"What shall I do to be saved?" But like the converted Paul, to ask, "Lord, what wilt thou have me to do?"

There are a great number of members in our churches, especially young converts with deep conviction, that believe the ordinances are in accordance with the teachings of God's Word. Yet, they need instruction as to the faith and practice of their denomination. These persons, perhaps, may have small means with which to purchase and little time to examine large books on the subject. Therefore, they desire to have the whole matter in a clear, condensed form.

The last six years of the author's life was spent as a general missionary, secretary, book agent, and publisher for the great National Baptist Convention.

Meeting and corresponding with churches, associations, and conventions in both cities and rural districts fully convinced him of the great need for Baptist churches to disseminate a plain, clear, concise, unadulterated scriptural doctrine.

Although there have been many denominational books published, there is a need for concise, detailed accounts of what Baptists believe. Therefore, it is absolutely necessary that *What Baptists Believe and Practice* should be printed. Such is the intention of the author in presenting this little pamphlet. He is not the writer of any of the subjects treated herein.

The Church Covenant and the eighteen Articles of Faith are taken from the *National Baptist Pastor's Guide*.

The article on Christian Baptism is a contribution by Rev. J. T. Brown, A.M., S.T.B.

The article on The Lord's Supper is from the pen of Rev. E. M. Brawley, D.D.

THE AUTHOR

CHURCH COVENANT

Having been led, as we believe, by the Spirit of God to receive the Lord Jesus Christ as our Savior; and on the profession of our faith, having been baptized in the name of the Father, and of the Son, and of the Holy Spirit, we do now in the presence of God, angels and this assembly, most solemnly and joyfully enter into covenant with one another, as one body in Christ.

We engage, therefore, by the aid of the Holy Spirit, to walk together in Christian love; to strive for the advancement of this church in knowledge and holiness; to give it a place in our affections, prayers and services above every organization of human origin; to sustain its worship, ordinances, discipline and doctrine; to contribute cheerfully and regularly, as God has prospered us, towards its expenses, for the support of a faithful and evangelical ministry among us, the relief of the poor and the spread of the Gospel throughout the world. In case of difference of opinion in the church, we will strive to avoid a contentious spirit, and if we cannot unanimously agree, we will cheerfully recognize the right of the majority to govern.

We also engage to maintain family and secret devotions; to study diligently the Word of God; to religiously educate our children; to seek the salvation of our kindred and acquaintances; to walk circumspectly in the world; to be kind and just to those in our employ, and faithful in the service we promise others; endeavoring in the purity of heart and good will towards all men to exemplify and commend our holy faith.

We further engage to watch over, to pray for, to exhort and stir up each other unto every good word and work; to guard each other's reputation, not needlessly exposing the infirmities of others; to participate in each other's joys, and with tender sympathy, bear one another's burdens and sorrows; to cultivate Christian courtesy; to be slow to give or take offense, but always ready for reconciliation, being mindful of the rules of the Savior in the eighteenth chapter of Matthew, to secure it without delay; and through life, amid evil report, and good report, to seek to live to the glory of God, who hath called us out of darkness into His marvelous light.

When we remove from this place, we engage as soon as possible, to unite with some other church, where we can carry out the spirit of this covenant and the principles of God's Word.

ARTICLES OF FAITH

The Articles of Faith which should be adopted by Baptist churches at the time of organization:

I. The Scriptures

We believe that the Holy Bible was written by men divinely inspired, and is a perfect treasure of heavenly instruction; that it has God for its author, salvation for its end, and truth without any mixture of error for its matter; that it reveals the principles by which God will judge us, and therefore is, and shall remain to the end of the world, the true center of Christian union, and the supreme standard by which all human conduct, creeds, and opinions shall be tried.

II. The True God

We believe the Scriptures teach that there is one, and only one, living and true God. An infinite, intelligent Spirit, whose name is Jehovah, the Maker and Supreme Ruler of heaven and earth; inexpressibly glorious in holiness, and worthy of all possible honor, confidence and love; that in the unity of the Godhead there are three persons, the Father, the Son, and the Holy Ghost; equal in every divine perfection, and executing distinct but harmonious offices in the great work of redemption.

III. The Fall of Man

We believe the Scriptures teach that man was created in holiness, under the law of his Maker; but by voluntary transgressions, fell from that holy and happy state; in consequence of which all men are now sinners, not by constraint but by choice; being by nature utterly void of that holiness required by the law of God, positively inclined to evil; and therefore under just condemnation to eternal ruin, without defense or excuse.

IV. The Way of Salvation

We believe the Scriptures teach that the salvation of sinners is wholly of grace; through the mediatorial offices of the Son of God; who by the appointment of the Father, freely took upon Him our nature, yet without sin; honored the divine law by His personal obedience, and by His death made a full atonement for our sins; that having risen from the dead, He is now enthroned in heaven, and uniting in His wonderful person the tenderest sympathies with divine perfections, He is in every way qualified to be a suitable, a compassionate, and an all-sufficient Savior.

V. Justification

We believe the Scriptures teach that the great Gospel blessing which Christ secures to such as believe in Him is justification; that justification includes the pardon of sin, and the promise of eternal life on principles of righteousness; that it is bestowed, not in consideration of any works of righteousness which we have done, but solely through faith in the Redeemer's blood; by virtue of which faith His perfect righteousness is freely imputed to us of God; that it brings us into a state of most blessed peace and favor with God, and secures every other blessing needful for time and eternity.

VI. The Freeness of Salvation

We believe the Scriptures teach that the blessings of salvation are made free to all by the Gospel. It is the immediate duty of all to accept them by cordial, penitent and obedient faith; and that nothing prevents the salvation of the greatest sinner on earth, but his own determined depravity and voluntary rejection of the Gospel. This rejection involves the sinner in an aggravated condemnation.

VII. Regeneration

We believe the Scriptures teach that in order to be saved, sinners must be regenerated, or born again.

Regeneration consists of giving a holy disposition to the mind; that it is effected in a manner above our comprehension by the power of the Holy Spirit, in connection with divine truth, so as to secure our voluntary obedience to the Gospel; and that its proper evidence appears in the holy fruits of repentance and faith, and newness of life.

VIII. Repentance and Faith

We believe the Scriptures teach that repentance and faith are sacred duties, and also inseparable graces wrought in our souls by the regenerating Spirit of God, whereby being deeply convinced of our guilt, danger and helplessness, and of the way of salvation by Christ, we turn to God with unfeigned contrition, confession, and supplication for mercy; at the same time, heartily receiving the Lord Jesus Christ as our prophet, priest, and king, and relying on Him alone as the only and all-sufficient Savior.

IX. God's Purpose of Grace

We believe the Scriptures teach that election is the eternal purpose of God, according to which He graciously regenerates, sanctifies and saves sinners; that being perfectly consistent with the free agency of man, it comprehends all the means in connection with the end; that it is a most glorious display of God's sovereign goodness, being infinitely free, wise, holy and unchangeable; that it utterly excludes boasting and promotes humility, love, prayer, praise, trust in God, and active imitation of His free mercy; that it encourages the use of means in the highest degree; that it may be ascertained by its effects in all who truly believe the Gospel; that it is the foundation of Christian assurance; and that to ascertain it with regard to ourselves, demands and deserves the utmost diligence.

X. Sanctification

We believe the Scriptures teach that sanctification is the process by which, according to the will of God, we are made partakers of His holiness; that it is a progressive work: that it is begun in regeneration; and that it is carried on in the hearts of believers by the presence and power of the Holy Spirit, the Sealer and Comforter, in the continual use of the appointed means—especially the Word of God, self-examination, self-denial, watchfulness, and prayer.

XI. Perseverance of Saints

We believe the Scriptures teach that such only are real believers as endure to the end; that their persevering attachment to Christ is the grand mark which distinguishes them from superficial professors; that a special providence watches over their welfare; and that they are kept by the power of God through faith unto salvation.

XII. The Law and Gospel

We believe the Scriptures teach that the Law of God is the eternal and unchangeable rule of His moral government; that it is holy, just, and good; and that the inability which the Scriptures ascribe to fallen men to fulfill its precepts, arises entirely from their love of sin. To deliver man from sin, and to restore him through a Mediator to unfeigned obedience to the Holy Law, is one great end óf the Gospel, and of the means of grace connected with the establishment of the visible church.

XIII. A Gospel Church

We believe the Scriptures teach that a visible church of Christ is a congregation of baptized believers, associated by covenant in the faith and fellowship of the Gospel, observing the ordinances of Christ, being governed by His laws, and exercising the gifts, rights, and privileges invested in them by His Word; that its only scriptural officers are bishops or pastors, and deacons, whose qualifications, claims and duties are defined in the Epistles to Timothy and Titus.

XIV. Baptism and the Lord's Supper

We believe the Scriptures teach that Christian baptism is the immersion in water of a believer, in the name of the Father, Son, and Holy Ghost, to show forth in a solemn and beautiful emblem, our faith in the crucified, buried, and risen Savior, with its effect shown in our death to sin and resurrection to a new life; that it is prerequisite to the privileges of a church relation, and to the Lord's Supper, in which the members of the church, by the sacred use of bread and wine, are to commemorate together the dying love of Christ, preceded always by solemn self-examination.

XV. The Christian Sabbath

We believe the Scriptures teach that the first day of the week is the Lord's Day, or Christian Sabbath, and is to be kept sacred for religious purpose, by abstaining from all secular labor and sinful recreations, by the devout observance of all the means of grace, both private and public, and by preparation for the rest that remaineth for the people of God.

XVI. Civil Government

We believe the Scriptures teach that civil government is of divine appointment, for the interest and good order of human society; and that magistrates are to be prayed for, conscientiously honored and obeyed, except only in things opposed to the will of our Lord Jesus Christ, who is the only Lord of the conscience, and the Prince of the Kings of the earth.

XVII. Righteous and Wicked

We believe the Scriptures teach that there is a radical and essential difference between the righteous and wicked; and that such only as through faith are justified in the name of the Lord Jesus, and sanctified by the Spirit of our God, are truly righteous in His esteem, while all such as continue in impenitence and unbelief are in His sight wicked, and under the curse; and this distinction holds among men both in and after death.

XVIII. The World to Come

We believe the Scriptures teach that the end of the world is approaching; that at the last day, Christ will descend from heaven, and raise the dead from the grave for final retribution; that a solemn separation will then take place; that the wicked will be adjudged to endless punishment, and the righteous to endless joy; and that this judgment will fix forever the final state of men in heaven or hell, on principles of righteousness.

CHRISTIAN BAPTISM

It may be asked, why do the Baptists, in their periodicals, conventional meetings and denominational books, keep the subject of Christian baptism so continually and forcefully before their own persuasion and the world?

The answer is, first, because it is necessary to teach the youth of our own great denomination, the fundamental doctrine of our denomination; and secondly, believing that we are right, it is our duty not to desist until we have converted our Pedobaptist brethren from the errors of their way.

It is just as reasonable to ask "Why do the teachers of our land continue to teach the fundamental principles of arithmetic to the children who apply to them for a knowledge of the science and the art of numbers?"

There is a vital principle of life beneath the contention for the real "Christian Baptism,"—the principle of absolute obedience. Upon this principle hangs life eternal.

The clear teaching of Jesus is: "Do this and thou shalt live: how shall we escape if we neglect so great salvation." The principle of obedience holds good, whether the command is issued under the law or under grace.

The chief difficulty of a question under debate rests in defining the meaning of the term containing the main idea controverted. The word which answers this description in the subject is "baptism." If we can reliably decide what is the authoritative and historical meaning of the word "baptize," we have virtually settled the controversy. A word is the sign of an idea. Frequently, the idea essential to an argument is contained in the meaning of a single word. The subject of Christian baptism is such a one.

With the meaning of this word, baptize, once scholarly and historically defined, the debate is at an end. Some other reason or excuse must be found for the palpable and willful ignoring of the evident and established meaning of the word.

Baptists believe that the Word of God is the only and sufficient guide for the world in matters of faith and practice. This belief is founded upon the presumption that the Bible is divinely inspired; that the God of creation is also the author of the library of sixty-six books, called the Bible; and that while He used men as His agents in the production of these books, without the destruction or suspension of their personalities, His omniscience and wisdom were used in the truth presented, and this omniscience and divine wisdom extended to the doctrine put forth and even the words selected to express these divine and ultra-human ideas.

A careful study of the doctrine of God's providence has left us the conclusion that the Greek language seems to have been created by this specially gifted and endowed people for the purpose of preparing a most flexible and perfect vehicle for the carrying of the "good news and glad tidings called the gospel."

When the Holy Spirit began the use of this language to convey the blessed truths of the Gospel, the supposition is fair and reasonable that He knew the import of each word in this language and the fitness of each one to convey certain ideas in His mind. Jesus Christ being divine, the very God, and John being sent to baptize, most likely knew the word appropriate to express the essential elements of baptism. The uniform and undeviating word is baptize.

Ecclesiastical history seems to have providentially kept the word intact in the Bible record, for as all the world now knows, the word baptize is not translated in our English version of the Bible, but is simply transferred to the English with the final "o" of the Greek changed to the "e" of the English to give it an English form. Thus, the meaning of this word is not to be found by consulting the English, but the Greek lexicons.

Consulting them, the uniform and unexceptional meaning is found to be, "to dip, to immerse, to immerse in water." There is not a single scholar in Christendom, whose reputation as such, is worth repeating, who does not affirm the truth of our statement.

The distinguished Pedobaptist scholars seemed to have held a convention for the express purpose of affirming the wisdom of the Holy Spirit in this matter and endorsing the Baptist position.

In 1889, the writer had the privilege of receiving the introduction of a native Greek who was studying theology in the famous Union Theological Seminary, in the city of New York, and was bold enough to ask him the primary conception of the word baptize in his language. Promptly he replied, that the word "*baptizo*" in his language had no other conception that to dip, or immerse in liquid. Other phases closely allied to this were expressed by other positive words, and that true to this idea the entire Greek church had never considered baptism anything but immersion.

Endorsing and corroborating this later day witness we have the testimony of such eminent leaders of Pedobaptism, as Professor Thayer of Harvard University, Moses Stuart, Westein, Calvin, Luther, Campbell, and a host of others too numerous to mention.

The place where baptism was performed and the plain declaration that it was performed by John in Enon, near Salim, because there was much water there, carry upon their face such conviction of truth that it can not be denied. That this may have always been renouncing the human substitutes for the baptism declaration contended for by the Baptists, is noteworthy. Who has ever in the history of his life read or heard of anyone baptized as the Baptists demand, who renounced his baptism and asked to be sprinkled, or poured as the result of Bible investigation and conscientious conviction? Show us such a one and we will show you a leaf in the forest upon which the wind has never blown, as Dr. Stokes would say.

Without effort to prove, we will simply state that the unbroken practice of the New Testament church for 250 years was uniformly that of dipping or immersion. And when the first innovation occurred in the case of Novatian, it was done over a written protest by his opponent who claimed Novatian "came not canonically to his orders, because it was not lawful for anyone that had been baptized in his bed in sickness to be admitted to any order of the clergy."

What is the design of Christian baptism? The answer to this question will help us to determine the nature of the things. As a rite, it must have some religious significance, or we must accuse Christ of accepting, endorsing and commanding a meaningless ordinance. This beautiful and simple ordinance was intended to each, pictorially, the death, burial and resurrection of the Savior and the believer's relation thereto. As such, only the immersion of the candidate in water can do this: everything else falls short of the great end for which the rite was evidently intended.

Sprinkling, pouring and other human devices fall far and utterly short of the ability to do this.

Baptism is a public inaugural act by which the candidate openly declares his allegiance to his newfound King and Master, and at the same time a sign of his severance of his relation with his former master. This he can and must do in the way the King himself had it done to him; the way he did it and the way he ordered it done. If he refuses, then he is found recreant in the first public duty imposed upon him by his king.

What does a king think of a subject who comes to him personally professing the greatest love and loyalty, but upon being ordered to perform his first public act of allegiance refuses to do it? Who are the subjects of baptism? The answer to this question separates the Baptists from all the rest of the Christian world. The

New Testament teaches that only intelligent and penitent believers are the subjects of baptism. The Bible contains God's remedy for sin—the plan of salvation. This gospel is addressed as a proposition to the intelligent, sentient creatures of earth. If God has any positive plan of salvation for infants, as such, he has not revealed it to us in the Bible.

The plan of salvation is an intelligent proposition of grace which Christ submits to man upon the strength of evident ability to reason, decide and regret. This is the general proposition: the special one with reference to baptism is that the Great Commission commands the church to preach and then baptize those who believe. Infants cannot believe and it is difficult to see why anyone should claim reasonableness in and be guilty of baptizing them. This was the condition of John's baptism, for the inspired record says: "Then went out to him Jerusalem and all Judea, and all the region round about Jordan and were baptized of him in Jordan, confessing their sins." Every instance of so-called household baptism has a phrase magnifying the idea of personal, conscious faith in the person baptized. The air of the sacred Scripture is charged with this truth; this impression is spontaneous; the common sense of mankind rises up in rebellion against the idea of reading infant baptism into the Scriptures. It simply is not there by express command; it is not there by example; it is not there by necessary inference.

The Romish Church claims the right to change ordinances; hence they decreed that sprinkling should be as valid as baptism. The Pedobaptist churches have simply accepted this perversion of Christ's doctrine from Rome, the fountain and source of the world's greatest spiritual errors. Baptists cannot and will not, claiming that all the laws necessary for the administration of His kingdom, Christ has made himself. Besides, the dangers of the kingdom are evident, since it admits unregenerated persons in Christ's kingdom as full members, thereby breaking a fundamental law which he taught to Nicodemus at the opening of his public ministry, viz., that except a man be born again, he cannot see the kingdom of God.

The baptism of infants is a serious innovation in the things of God. It is said that the great Henry Ward Beecher used to say openly when sprinkling babies: "I practice infant sprinkling because I think it is a good thing, and not because the New Testament commands it."

Herein he and the whole Pedobaptist world differ from the Baptists. They believe in substituting their opinions for the plain Word of God. The Baptists believe in teaching the believers to observe all things whatsoever He has commanded us, and then stop.

There is an idea prevalent among some Baptists who claim to be "liberal" that any one is qualified to perform the ordinance of baptism if he only holds membership and communion in some evangelical church. We hold the view most consistent with reason and denominational custom. We do hold that persons coming to regular Baptist churches who have been baptized by denominations that do not hold the same strict and close view about baptism as we, ought to be baptized. Why? Not because we consider the administrator essential to the baptismal act but because we consider a proper administrator, one who has been baptized by one who believes in the form and spirit of the Bible baptism, necessary to preserve the soundness of the atmosphere around the act.

In order to prevent the creeping into the church of Christ, of those little inconsistencies that, like "the little foxes," gnaw and destroy the beauty, health and fruitfulness of the vine, we rebaptize the candidate on the same principle that we re-ordain the man who baptized him when he, as a gospel minister, seeks a place in our pulpit. It is not because we doubt his essential knowledge of the Bible doctrine of salvation, but to find out if his knowledge and belief as a whole corresponds to the doctrines of grace as the Baptists see them—to preserve the unity of faith and practice commanded by the Holy Spirit.

If it is in the interest of truth to re-examine it and re-ordain the Pedobaptist preacher who becomes a Baptist, we cannot see why it is considered hard or inconsistent to rebaptize his Pedobaptist candidate. If we condemn the workman, how can we endorse his work? We must either make the tree good and the fruit evil. Thus, we believe that the Baptists are impregnable in their positions respecting the doctrines, in spite of the tendency of some of our brethren to fly off into what the worldly-minded scholarship calls "liberalism."

Baptists are not one whit behind in that deep and broad scholarship that crowns the brow of genius, and because of this fact are more firmly rooted in the essential correctness and general consistency of our position. We are more careful to be Scriptural than "liberal."

There is not much doubt that these questions will continue to be discussed until they are settled right, for "nothing is ever settled until it is settled right."

The drift of the matter, "the beginning of the end," is seen in the increasing readiness with which all denominations now baptize by immersion.

Time was when it was an insult for a candidate to request a Pedobaptist minister to immerse him, but now these same ministers in Baptist strongholds ask the candidates how they wish to be baptized—by immersion or sprinkling, etc.? This is the result of the Baptists' faithful and aggressive contending for the "one Lord, one faith and one baptism." May the Spirit of the Lord breathe upon these slain that they may stand up a mighty army, battling for the truth as it shines in the face of Jesus Christ.

As it lies mysteriously though powerfully concealed and revealed in the beautiful emblem of Christian Baptism, sacred enough for Christ to accept, sublime enough to claim the Spirit's presence and endorsement, dignified enough to cause the Father's voice to break the silence of eternity in His ratification, and righteous enough to extort from Christ, our Master, the last argument that can be made for the rite—a necessity for righteousness.

DOCTRINE OF THE LORD'S SUPPER

SECTION I

Institution and Perpetuity

The rite which we usually call the Lord's Supper was instituted by our Savior on the night before his death. He intended it to be observed by His churches until the end of time. "The Lord's Supper is that outward rite in which the assembled church eats bread and drinks wine poured forth by its appointed representative, in token of its constant dependence on the once crucified, now risen Savior. It is a source of spiritual life or, in other words a token of that abiding communication of Christ's death and resurrection through which the life begun in regeneration is sustained and perfected." (*Strong: Systematic Theology*, pp. 538–539).

Notice in this definition the following propositions:

1. The Supper is an established ordinance.

2.   It is to be observed by the assembled church.

3.   The elements used are bread and wine.

4.   It is commemorative of Christ's death.

Four of the sacred writers describe the institution of the Supper namely, Matthew 26:26-39; Mark 14:22–25; Luke 22:17–20; and Paul—1 Corinthians 11:23–26. From these accounts we learn that at the close of the last paschal supper which Jesus observed with the twelve, He instituted this tender and impressive memorial. It was to be observed after His death, for only after His death could it be commemorative; and its observance was to continue until His Second Coming.

Unlike baptism, which is to be administered once only to the believer, the Supper is to be taken at regular intervals in token of our constant dependence on Jesus, once crucified but now risen and exalted, who is the source of our spiritual life.

Luke 22:19 — "And he took bread, and gave thanks, and brake it, and gave unto them, saying, This is my body which is given for you: this do in remembrance of me."

First Corinthians 11:23–26 — "For I have received of the Lord that which also I delivered unto you. That the Lord Jesus the same night in which he was betrayed took bread: And when he had given thanks, he brake it, and said, Take, eat: this is my body, which is broken for you: this do in remembrance of me. After the same manner also he took the cup, when he had supped, saying, This cup is the new testament in my blood: this do ye, as oft as ye drink it, in remembrance of me. For as often as ye eat this bread, and drink this cup, ye do shew the Lord's death till he come."

Acts 2:42, 46 — "And they continued steadfastly in the apostles' doctrine and fellowship, and in breaking of bread, and in prayers…. And they, continuing daily with one accord in the temple, and breaking bread from house to house, did eat their meat with gladness and singleness of heart."

Acts 20:7 — "And upon the first day of the week, when the disciples came together to break bread, Paul preached unto them."

The Lord's Supper is to be observed by the assembled church, for both the ordinances were committed to the entire church to be observed and guarded.

Matthew 28:19–20 — "Go ye therefore, and teach all nations, baptizing them in the name of the Father, and of the Son, and of the Holy Ghost: Teaching them to observe all things whatsoever I have commanded you."

Luke 24:33 — "And they rose up the same hour, and returned to Jerusalem, and found the eleven gathered together, and them that were with them."

Acts 1:15 — "And in those days Peter stood up in the midst of the disciples, and said, (the number of names together were about an hundred and twenty)."

First Corinthians 15:6 — "After than, he was seen of above five hundred brethren at once."

These passages show that it was not to the eleven apostles alone that Christ committed the ordinances; it being remembered that the Great Commission (Matthew 28:19,20) was not given on Olivet at the time of the ascension, when only the eleven were present, but on the mountain in Galilee at the great meeting which Jesus had appointed (Matthew 26:32; 28:7,10).

More than five hundred brethren were gathered, not counting the women who were probably also present and more numerous. For this reason, then, the ordinances belong to the church and not to individuals. Notice Paul's statement to the church at Corinth (1 Corinthians 11:2): "Now I praise you, brethren, that ye remember me in all things, and keep the ordinances, as I delivered them to you."

The elements of the Supper were bread and wine, the former being unleavened and the latter may have been fermented. But we are not now required to use unleavened bread and fermented wine. Mere bread, whether leavened or unleavened, and wine, fermented or unfermented, are the things needed. Hence it is proper for us to use unfermented wine, and it is better to do so. Broadus (*Commentary on Matthew*, page 528): "It (the bread) was unleavened, of course, as required by the law at the passover; but our Lord makes no reference to this, and it is not wise to insist on using only unleavened bread in the Lord's Supper."

Hovey (*Systematic Theology*, page 334): "The bread was doubtless unleavened; yet this peculiarity is nowhere referred to by the sacred writers, or by Christ himself and hence is not to be looked upon as significant." Strong (*Systematic Theology*, page 539): "Although the wine which Jesus poured out was doubtless the ordinary fermented juice of the grape, there is nothing in the symbolism of the ordinance which forbids the use of unfermented juice of grape. Obedience to the command, 'This do in remembrance of me,' requires only that we shall use the 'fruit of the vine.'"

At the institution of the Supper only the faithful eleven were present. Judas was not, as he had left the room toward the close of the paschal meal, before the institution of the supper, and had gone to the chief priests for the purpose of betraying Jesus. It seems strange to us that Jesus did not invite Mary Magdalene, Joanna, Susanna (Luke 8:1–3) and other faithful disciples to the Supper; but he did not do so, and doubtless he had good reasons for his decision not to have them present.

As to the frequency of the celebration of the Supper it may be remarked that we have no uniform Scripture precedent. A sound discretion in this matter is to be exercised. The early church sometimes administered the ordinance daily, and then again weekly. Perhaps for us this would be too frequent. And, yet, once in three months—the custom of some churches—is too seldom. Probably once a month may be frequent enough.

SECTION II

Name

Various names are in common use to designate this ordinance. It is sometimes spoken of as the Lord's Supper, the Eucharist, and the Communion. The Scriptural designation of the ordinance is the Breaking of Bread

(Acts 2:43; 20:7), but this is seldom, almost never used. The expression—Lord's Supper—is used once only (1 Corinthians 11:20). But while we usually interpret these words as meaning this rite, yet it is not certain that they do refer to it since some expositors think that they mean the love feast, which was celebrated in connection with it. However, the weight of present testimony is in favor of the current view; and if this be correct, then once, and once only, in the New Testament is the ordinance named. The Lord's Supper is an expressive phrase, since the rite was instituted by our Lord.

The name Eucharist is sometimes used, but it does not occur in Scripture. It is derived from the Greek word *Eucharisteo*, which means to give thanks, and refers to the thanksgiving which preceded the distribution of the bread and wine. If the thanksgiving were the principal thing in the celebration of the ordinance, then Eucharist would be a good name for it, but the essential thing is remembering Jesus, and some name should be used which will keep the fact steadily before us. Baptists very seldom use the word Eucharist.

Perhaps the name in most common use among us is Communion, and it is the one with the least authority behind it. Burrows (*Popular Objections to Baptist Principles*, p. 29), says: "The Greek word *koinonia*, which we sometimes translate Communion, occurs in just twenty different places in the New Testament; in twelve, translated 'fellowship'; in one, 'distribution'; in one, 'contribution'; in four, 'communion'; and in only two of all, and both in the same passage, it is used with any reference to the Lord's Supper. The word Communion, in its proper signification in New Testament usage, is equivalent to agreement, fellowship."

It thus keeps entirely out of view the great design of the ordinance, and presents as its chief idea the fellowship of believers. Now it is perfectly right to remember that believers are in Christian fellowship, but the Lord's Supper was not instituted for that end. And it is probable that this wrong use of the word communion is largely responsible for the very general ignorance which prevails concerning the design of the ordinance, and for the notion that all Christians should sit together at the Lord's Table.

Broadus comments: "The Lord's Supper is often called the 'Communion' through misunderstanding of 1 Corinthians 10:16, where the word communion really means 'participation,' as in *Revised Version* margin. This wrong name for the ordinance has often proved misleading." Substitute 'participation,' as the margin suggests and 1 Corinthians 10:16 in the *Revised Version* would read: "The cup of blessing which we bless, is it not a participation in the blood of Christ?

The bread which we break, is it not a participation in the body of Christ?" Remember now that twice only is the Greek work *koinonia*, which we ordinarily translate 'communion,' used in reference to the Lord's Supper, and that the two instances are in the verse just quoted, in which 'participation' in both cases is the more correct translation. We conclude that the name communion utterly lacks the support of Scripture, and is hence not a proper designation of the sacred ordinance, and therefore should not be used at all. Baptists have nothing to lose and everything to gain by standing close to the Scriptures, and avoiding everything that savors of tradition. In this way they secured their great victories in the past, and in this same way they will make greater triumphs in the future.

SECTION III

Current Views

The differences existing among Christians as to their doctrines and ordinances are clearly set forth in their printed documents, and there is no possibility of mistaking any one of them for another; but it is not so in current belief and practice. The duties and amenities of social life, whereby people belonging to denominations of widely different views are daily thrown together in pleasant intercourse, cause a general mixing of religious views.

It is not a strange thing to find a Methodist who associates with a Presbyterian holding Calvinistic views of the atonement, and the Presbyterian endorsing Armenian views of the same doctrine. And so, many Baptists who associate constantly with Methodists are practically Armenian on the great doctrines of grace. Hence it is not remarkable to find people who ought to have well-defined views as to the Lord's Supper, standing at all points between Transubstantiation of the Catholic Church and the simple Zwinglian doctrine as held by Baptists. True, this mixture of truth with error is due largely to a lack of thorough Bible teaching, but it is also attributable to the influence of personal friendships. It must also be admitted that any system of religious truth is most radical and pronounced where there is least opposition to it. Hence Presbyterianism is clearest and strongest in Scotland, and Catholicism shows its true features in strictly Roman Catholic countries.

We need not, therefore, wonder when we find some Baptists tainted with sacramental notions concerning the

Lord's Supper. It could hardly be otherwise. And for this reason there is great need of stating and restating the Bible teaching on this rite.

There are four prominent views held and taught by Christians at the present time concerning the Lord's Supper.

The first is the doctrine of Transubstantiation, held by the Catholic Church. It is "that the bread and wine are changed by priestly consecration into the very body and blood of Christ; that this consecration is a new offering of Christ's sacrifice; and that by a physical partaking of the elements, the communicant receives saving grace from God." This doctrine is, of course, unscriptural.

1. *It virtually denies the completeness of Christ's past sacrifice.*

Hebrews 7:27—"Who needeth not daily, as those high priests, to offer up sacrifice, first for his own sins, and then for the people's: for this he did once, when he offered up himself."

Hebrews 9:26, 28—"For then must he often have suffered since the foundation of the world: but now once in the end of the world hath he appeared to put away sin by the sacrifice of himself. So Christ was once offered to bear the sins of many."

Hebrews 10:10—"By the which will we are sanctified through the offering of the body of Jesus Christ once for all." Christ thus offered himself a sacrifice once; and the act is final and will never be repeated.

2. It makes the Lord's Supper a sacrament, which is a mysterious something, supposed to be the vehicle of grace.

Sacramentum means primarily an oath, and hence anything sacred. As used in Catholicism, "A sacrament is something presented to the senses, which has the power, by divine institution, not only of signifying, but also sufficiently conveying grace."

Episcopalians teach that "sacraments instituted by Christ are not only the badges and tokens of the profession of the Christian men, but rather they be certain sure witnesses and effectual signs of grace." Presbyterians, Methodists and Pedobaptists, generally, all teach substantially the same thing, namely, that the Lord's Supper is a sacrament. Baptists repudiate the notion that the Supper is a sacrament, for they find no authority in Scripture for regarding it as the vehicle of grace. And hence we should never speak of the Lord's Supper and baptism as sacraments, but only as symbols that powerfully teach truth. The supper is a simple memorial devoid of all mystical and magical power.

3. *This error of Transubstantiation rests upon a false interpretation of God's Word.*

When Jesus said "Take, eat; this is my body," (Matthew 26:26) he spoke in a plain, common sense way, expecting the eleven to understand him, and they doubtless did. They knew that the bread was not the real body of Jesus, but represented it. So in verse 28, the same chapter, Jesus said, "This is my blood of the new testament, which is shed." No one in his good sense could understand Jesus as meaning that the wine was literal blood, and was already shed, for he had not yet suffered death. That this bread represented His body, and the wine represents His blood, is the Savior's meaning, just as when Jesus said (John 15:5) "I am the vine." He meant to show that He was the source of spiritual life.

The second current view is that know as Consubstantiation. This is the Lutheran view. It is "that the communicant, in partaking of the consecrated elements, eats the veritable body and drinks the veritable blood of Christ in and with the bread and wine, although the elements themselves do not cease to be material."

Luther invented this name and doctrine in his reaction against Roman Catholicism and Transubstantiation. The following quotation is from his catechism: "Question: What is now the sacrament of the altar? Answer: It is the true body and blood of the Lord Christ, in and under the bread and wine which we Christians are through Christ's word commanded to eat and to drink...but how the body is in the bread, we know not."

This view, like the preceding, is also unscriptural. It is based upon a literal interpretation of language that Christ evidently meant to be figurative, and it leads to gross absurdity. Moreover, it contradicts the doctrine of justification only by faith, and converts a mere symbol into means of salvation.

This third view is the one now held by Episcopalians, Presbyterians, and Methodists. It is, "that to the partaking of the bread is attached by divine appointment a special spiritual blessing, which is received by all who take the bread in faith and which cannot be had without taking it." Thus it will be seen that these denominations also make the Lord's Supper a sacrament.

The fourth view, the one held generally by Baptists, is that "the bread is simply appointed as the symbol or memento, which we take in remembrance of the Savior's body, and that the natural effect of such a memento or symbol in vividly remembering the Savior, and kindling grateful affection toward him, is a blessing to the devout participant. But the blessing thus received is not supposed to be essentially different in kind from other spiritual blessings, or to be associated by mere divine appointment with this particular means of grace." With this view of the ordinance, it is nonsense, rather a contradiction for Baptists to use the word sacrament.

That there should be widely divergent views among Christians at the present time concerning the ordinance of the Lord's Supper is but natural, for early in the history of the Christian church the ordinances were corrupted. The true scriptural baptism, which was immersion only, was set aside by many Christians, and pouring and sprinkling substituted; and from being a mere symbol of the burial and resurrection of Jesus, baptism was regarded as the instrument of regeneration.

The Lord's Supper was similarly perverted and made a sacrament—the vehicle of bringing a certain spiritual blessing which could be obtained in no other way. The Reformers of the sixteenth century, while making wonderful strides as to the great doctrines of grace, particularly justification by faith, were hopelessly at sea as to the ordinances. Beckett (*The Reformation in England*, p. 136) says: "The great topic of doctrinal controversy among Protestants was concerning the Sacraments.

Luther, in most points the boldest, the most spiritual of the Reformers, on the subject of the Sacraments was most hesitant. In the water of baptism he believed an actual change took place, so that it was no longer water, but had the power of the blood of Christ." In reference to the bread and wine of the Lord's Supper he taught under the name of 'Consubstantiation', a corporeal real presence of the body and blood of Christ, thus giving, as has been observed, 'a fresh lease on life' to the old dogma of Transubstantiation.

To the clear-headed and intrepid Zwingli more than any other of the Reformers is the Protestant church indebted for a doctrine at once more rational and spiritual. Had the Reformers been as clear-sighted and as bold concerning the ordinances as they were concerning the great doctrines, baptism would have been restored to its rightful, scriptural place, and Protestant Christendom would not now be divided over the ordinance.

SECTION IV

Import and Design

Many things in Christ's life are supremely important, as His incarnation, baptism, temptation, preaching and transfiguration, but the Lord's Supper has nothing whatever to do with any of them. It was given to be mainly a memorial of Christ's death but it likewise shows the union of the believer with Christ and his constant dependence upon Christ for the sustenance of his spiritual life, and also the future blessedness of believers in the presence of Christ at the marriage supper of the Lamb.

1. *It is a memorial of Christ, hence it is not the real body and blood of Christ, nor yet a sacrament to bring grace.*

First Corinthians 11:24-26—"And when he had given thanks, he brake it, and said, Take, eat: this is my body, which is broken for you: this do in remembrance of me. After the same manner also he took the cup, when he had supped, saying, This cup is the new testament in my blood: this do ye, as oft as ye drink it, in remembrance of me. For as often as ye eat this bread and drink this cup, ye do shew the Lord's death till he come." The emblems, though mere bread and wine, while not at all vehicles of grace, are nevertheless powerful reminders of what Jesus did to deliver us from the bondage and penalty of sin just as the paschal supper of the Jews was a constant memorial to them of their deliverance from bondage of Egypt.

We all know from experience how powerful the simplest memorials of departed loved ones are in moving our hearts and bringing afresh to memory their words and deeds. It is important that we shall always keep in mind and teach the simple memorial character of the Lord's Supper, since so many Baptists have unconsciously received from their Pedobaptist associates the notion that some spiritual efficacy attends the administration of this rite.

2. *It shows the union of the believer with Christ, and his constant dependence upon Christ for the sustenance of his spiritual life.*

In regeneration the individual becomes united to Christ, and then receives spiritual life. But he is but a branch and Christ is the vine, and, "As the branch cannot bear fruit of itself, except it abide in the vine; no more can ye, except ye abide in me" (John 15:4). So also John 6-53: "Verily, verily I say unto you, Except ye eat the flesh of the Son of man, and drink his blood, ye have no life in you."

Christ is not here speaking of the Lord's Supper, but of spiritual union with Himself symbolized by the Lord's Supper, and His language is of course figurative, as is shown by verse 63, of the same chapter: "The flesh profiteth nothing: the words that I speak unto you, they are spirit, and they are life."

3. It also shows the future blessedness of believers in the presence of Christ at the marriage supper of the Lamb.

Some theologians have doubted that the Lord's Supper symbolizes the future blessedness of believers, but that is the clear meaning of Matthew 26:29: "But I say unto you, I will not drink hence forth of this fruit of the vine, until that day when I drink it new with you in my Father's kingdom." It will be remembered that we are to keep this ordinance only until Jesus returns, when His kingdom will be fully established. Then will come true the words of Revelation 19:7–9, "Let us be glad and rejoice, and give honor to him: for the marriage of the Lamb is come, and his wife hath made herself ready. And to her was granted that she should be arrayed in fine linen, clean and white: for the fine linen is the righteousness of saints. And he saith unto me Write, Blessed are they which are called unto the marriage supper of the Lamb."

The language is highly figurative. The wife represents the redeemed out of every nation, often called the church universal, and the Lamb is Jesus Christ, now triumphant. "The elect church, the heavenly bride, soon after the destruction of the harlot, is transfigured at the Lord's coming and joins with him in his triumph over the beast.

Perfect union with Him personally, and participation in His holiness, joy, glory and kingdom are included in the symbol 'marriage'."

SECTION V

Qualifications of Participants

Those who desire to partake of the Lord's Supper must possess certain qualifications. There is and can be no discussion about this, for no denomination would admit to the Lord's Table men regardless of their character. Some qualifications are absolutely required, and it is worthy of remark that all Protestant Christians agree substantially in stating what they are.

1. The first and fundamental qualification of the participant is the possession of saving faith. He must be a regenerated believer.

If he is not how can he "remember Jesus"? Or why should he be one of a company who take the symbols of bread and wine which show that these believers draw spiritual life from Christ if he has no spiritual life? Or how can such a man "discern the Lord's body"? Clearly, regeneration is the first qualification.

2. The second qualification is baptism. Baptism is the door into the church, and it cannot otherwise be entered.

Evangelical Christians generally insist on this as the second qualification, even though they charge us with what is called "Closed Communion."

Dr. Schaff, the eminent Presbyterian, (*Church History, Volume 1*, page 392) says: "The Communion was a regular, and, in fact, the most important and solemn part of the Sunday worship."

Bishop Coxe, Episcopal, (*Sermon on Christian Unity*), says: "The Baptists hold that we have never been baptized, and they must exclude us from their communion table, if we were disposed to go there. Are we offended? No. We call it principle, and we respect it. To say that we have never become members of Christ by baptism is severe, but it is conscientious adherence to duty as they regard it. I should be the bigot, and not they, if I should ask them to violate their discipline in this or in any other particular."

Dr. Hibbard, a very prominent Methodist scholar (*Christian Baptism*, part 2, page 174), says: "In one principle Baptist and Pedobaptist churches agree. They both agree in rejecting from communion at the Table of the Lord, and in denying the rights of church fellowship, all who have not been baptized. The charge of closed communion is not more applicable to the Baptists than to us (Pedobaptist), insomuch as the question of church fellowship with them is determined by as liberal principles as it is with any other Protestant church. I mean as the present subject is concerned (i.e., it is determined by valid baptism)."

The Congregational, in an editorial, July 9, 1879, says: "Congregationalists have uniformly, until here and there an exception has arisen of late years, required baptism and church membership as the prerequisite of a seat at the table of the Lord. It is a part of the false 'liberality' which now prevails in certain quarters to welcome everybody who thinks he loves Christ to commune in His body and blood. Such a course is the first step in breaking down that distinction between the church and the world which our Savior emphasized and it seemed to us that it is an unwise and mistaken act for which no Scripture warrant exists."

These extracts from leading Pedobaptist scholars might be multiplied. As to demanding baptism and church membership as qualifications for the Lord's Supper, there is remarkable agreement among Christians of all names. So that the thing called Closed Communion as applied to Baptists is a myth. But there is a difference, and that is concerning what is valid baptism.

Holding as we do that immersion only is baptism, we cannot accept as baptized any Pedobaptist who has been sprinkled. But they can accept us to their table because they recognize our baptism as valid. The entire difficulty now existing as to the admission of our Pedobaptist friends to the Lord's Table is simply a question as to what is valid baptism. Standing squarely on God's Word, we can accept nothing as baptism but immersion for that and that only is the baptismal act.

3. The third qualification for the Supper is an orderly and consistent Christian life.

He whose life is morally wrong is of course unfit to partake of the Supper. Anyone guilty of creating divisions in the church, or teaching heresy, or is guilty of covetousness, which is idolatry, is likewise unfit, for all such people deserve to be excluded from the church.

It is not enough for a man to believe truth; he must live it, and an orderly and consistent Christian life demands that every force at his command shall be exerted against error.

The following extract from Hiscox's *The New Directory for Baptist Churches*, pp. 452, 453, is a fitting close to this chapter. "Baptists give the following reasons in justification of their course in the following cases:

a. They do not invite Pedobaptist to their Communion because they do not regard such persons as baptized; they have been only sprinkled. The fact that they think themselves baptized does not make it so. If they desire to commune, let them be baptized according to Christ's command.

b. They do not accept invitations from Pedobaptists to commune with them for the same reason; they do not consider them baptized Christians. Therefore, their churches are irregular churches according to the New Testament standard, both in the misuse of the ordinances and in the admission of infant church membership. Therefore, to commune with them would be disorderly walking, and would encourage them in this disorderly walking, by upholding a perversion of the ordinances.

c. They do not invite the immersed members of Pedobaptist churches to their Communion, because though such persons may be truly converted and properly baptized, they are walking disorderly as disciples, by remaining in churches which hold and practice serious errors as the ordinances. These churches use sprinkling for baptism, and administer the ordinance to infants; both of which are contrary to Scripture. And yet, by remaining in these churches they give their countenance and support to uphold and perpetuate what they confess to be errors, and thus help to impose on others what they will not accept for themselves. This is not any orderly and consistent course for Christians to pursue."

SECTION VI

Some Popular Errors

As at the very beginning some wrong practices were indulged in at the celebration of the Lord's Supper, so all along the centuries errors more or less serious have clung to it. Some of these have already been mentioned. It is now proposed to mention a few current ones of a very popular character which are believed by Baptists.

1. *The first one is the belief that when a given quantity of wine has been brought into the church for the celebration of the Supper, every drop of it must be used.*

This error is the result of a wrong interpretation of Matthew 26–27, "Drink ye all of it." The word "all" is supposed to refer to the wine; but this is manifestly wrong, since the Greek Testament plains shows that "all" is in the nominative case, and is in apposition with the subject of the verb. And so the meaning is, "All ye drink of it." We are not commanded to drink all the wine, only as much of it as is needed for a proper observance of the ordinance. This error is met in a great many places. The writer has seen many instances when, after the conclusion of the Supper, the deacons and a few of the leading brethren and sisters would assemble for the purpose of drinking all the remaining wine, and as a result a condition of affairs was produced that closely resembled the serious errors that Paul sought to correct in the church at Corinth.

2. Another popular error is that concerning "drinking damnation."

Had this error been the truth, it would be now an exceedingly serious matter for many people, for they would be in torment. First Corinthians 11:29, reads, "For he that eateth and drinketh unworthily, eateth and drinketh damnation to himself, not discerning the Lord's body." Many people believe that if they partake of the Lord's Supper when they are too unworthy to do so, they will be damned. First of all, this error grows out of the word "damnation," which is an old English word whose current meaning is condemnation, or better still, judgment.

It does not mean being consigned to hell. Great stress has been placed on the word "unworthily," which is an adverb and refers to the manner of partaking of the Supper, and it has been read as if it were an adjective and referred to the character of the participants. Now, the truth is that the best Greek text omits the word.

The Revised Version translates the verse: "For he that eateth and drinketh, eateth and drinketh judgment unto himself, if he discern (discriminate) not the body." The *Bible Union Translation* is: "For he that eats and drinks, eat and drinks judgment to himself, if he discern not the body."

It will be noticed that not only is the word "unworthily" omitted, but also the word "Lord's." This is in conformity with all the leading textual critics. Paul meant in this passage to say that as the Corinthian church had practically failed to recognize the symbolism of the elements, bread and wine, had treated the ordinance as a common meal, and they were guilty of an unbecoming act.

3.   *The third error noticed is that we shall eat the Lord's Supper in heaven.*

It is founded on a false interpretation of Matthew 26:29: "But I say unto you, I will not drink henceforth of this fruit of the vine, until that day when I drink it new with you in my Father's kingdom." The best interpretation of this figurative passage is that given by Broadus: "Jesus has gradually succeeded in making it plain to them that he will not establish a temporal kingdom, such as the Jews expected the Messiah to found. He is going to die; will soon leave them.

But there will be a future kingdom of God, not a temporal, but a spiritual kingdom, in which all things will be new. In the New Kingdom, founded on the New Covenant, he will meet them again, and drink with them a new kind of wine. This can hardly be understood otherwise than as a figure."

It should be remembered that the Lord's Supper is given that we might always keep Jesus in remembrance. After His return, we shall be "forever with the Lord"; therefore, such a memorial will not be needed. Paul expressly tells us that we are to keep the ordinance only "till he comes." So there will not be any celebration of the Lord's Supper in heaven, for the necessity of it will have passed away when we shall permanently dwell with Jesus.

NOTES

_____

_____

_____

_____

_____

_____

_____

_____

_____

_____

_____

_____

_____

_____

_____

_____

_____

_____

_____

_____

NOTES

NOTES

NOTES

NOTES

NOTES

_____

_____

_____

_____

_____

_____

_____

_____

_____

_____

_____

_____

_____

_____

_____

_____

_____

_____

_____

_____

NOTES